# Where Do the Puddles Go?

## David Tunkin

It has rained and there are puddles on the ground.

3

The sun comes out and the water in the puddles starts to dry up. Where does the water go?

Heat from the sun can make water evaporate. When water evaporates, it turns into water vapor. We cannot see water vapor, but it is in the air.

As warm air rises, it cools. The water vapor in the air cools, too. When water vapor cools enough, it condenses. This means water vapor turns into tiny drops of water. The drops of water can form clouds.

In the clouds, the water drops join together. The clouds are made of big water drops. The clouds get darker.

These big water drops can get too heavy to stay in the clouds. The drops fall as rain. The rain can make puddles.

Soon the sun will make the water in the puddles evaporate again. The movement of water from the ground into the air and back to the ground again is called the water cycle.

**3** Water vapor condenses. Clouds are made.

**2** Water evaporates. It turns into water vapor.

**4** Water in the clouds falls as rain.

15

# Glossary

**condense**      when water vapor changes into water

**evaporate**      when water changes into water vapor

**water cycle**      movement of water from the ground into the air and back to the ground

**water vapor**      water that has evaporated; it is in the air but you cannot see it

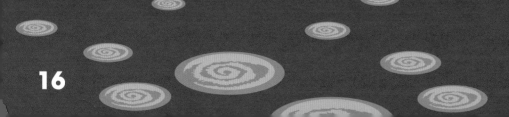